A TRUE BOOK

W9-CDO-184

Cyberbullying

LUCIA RAATMA

Children's Press®
An Imprint of Scholastic Inc.
New York   Toronto   London   Auckland   Sydney
Mexico City   New Delhi   Hong Kong
Danbury, Connecticut

Content Consultants

Dave Riley, PhD, is a professor in the Human Development & Family Studies Department at the University of Wisconsin–Madison. Colette Sisco is a faculty member in the Psychology Department at Madison College in Madison, Wisonsin.

Library of Congress Cataloging-in-Publication Data

Raatma, Lucia.
  Cyberbullying/by Lucia Raatma.
    p. cm.—(A true book)
  Includes bibliographical references and index.
  ISBN 978-0-531-25522-3 (library binding) — ISBN 978-0-531-23922-3 (pbk.)
 1. Cyberbullying—Juvenile literature. 2. Cyberbullying—Prevention—Juvenile literature. I. Title.
  HV6773.15.C92R33 2013
  302.34'302854678—dc23   2012036048

All rights reserved. Published in 2013 by Children's Press, an imprint of Scholastic Inc.
Printed in the United States of America 113
SCHOLASTIC, CHILDREN'S PRESS, A TRUE BOOK™, and associated logos are trademarks and/or registered trademarks of Scholastic Inc.
1 2 3 4 5 6 7 8 9 10 R 22 21 20 19 18 17 16 15 14 13

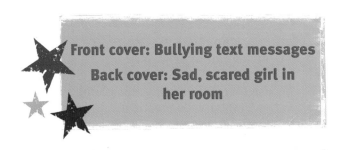

Front cover: Bullying text messages
Back cover: Sad, scared girl in her room

Find the Truth!

Everything you are about to read is true *except* for one of the sentences on this page.

Which one is **TRUE**?

T or F   Not all social media sites are suitable for users of all ages.

T or F   You always know who is talking when someone sends a message or posts online.

Find the answers in this book.

Contents

1 Understanding Cyberbullying

Where does cyberbullying happen? 7

2 Why Cyberbullying Is So Serious

What are the effects of cyberbullying? 17

THE BIG TRUTH!

Bullying Can Happen 24/7

How is cyberbullying different from being
bullied at school? 24

3 How to Handle Cyberbullying

Where can a victim find help? 27

4

Cyberbullying sometimes leads to bullying in person.

4 Ways to Stop Cyberbullying

What can victims say or do when they are cyberbullied? 35

True Statistics 44

Resources 45

Important Words 46

Index 47

About the Author 48

Computer use can be fun when there is no cyberbullying!

Being cyberbullied can be frightening and hurtful.

CHAPTER 1

Understanding Cyberbullying

Has anyone ever sent a mean text message to you? Or has a person ever **posted** something negative about you or a friend online? Cyberbullying is when someone is repeatedly threatened or embarrassed by another person online. This could happen on the Internet or through cell phones. Cyberbullies want to feel more powerful or more important than another person.

 Cyberbullying is a series of incidents, not a one-time thing.

Bullying by E-mail or Text

These days, most kids have access to e-mail accounts and texting. These services are fun and easy to use, but some people misuse them. Cyberbullies might send e-mails that tease or **taunt** other people. They might say hurtful things in an e-mail such as, "I hate you, and so does everyone else."

E-mail is great for keeping in touch with friends and family. But it is sometimes misused by cyberbullies.

Many cyberbullies have been bullied face-to-face. They go online to bully other people.

Text messages are fast. They come through almost instantly. Cyberbullies might send text messages that are threatening or mean. These messages could be something like, "I know where you live. You can't avoid me." Bullies might send them over and over. If you are the **victim** of a cyberbully, these messages may seem like they never stop. If a victim relies on his cell phone, he may feel like he can't escape the mean comments.

Tripping in the cafeteria can be embarrassing enough. Finding a photo or video of it posted online for the whole school to see can be even worse.

Bullying on Web Sites and Blogs

Some people create Web sites to talk about themselves or their hobbies. Other people create Web sites just to taunt people. These cyberbullies might post embarrassing photos and write negative comments about the people they target. Maybe someone slipped and fell in the cafeteria. An embarrassing photo of that can be posted online for everyone to see.

Blogs are like online journals. Many people use them like diaries to write about their lives and feelings. However, some people use blogs to bully other people. These bloggers might write long entries that criticize or spread **rumors** about people. They might make fun of what people wear or how they look. Unlike a diary in a notebook, a blog is online and can be read by anyone.

The most common forms of cyberbullying are posting hurtful comments and spreading rumors.

Have you ever found a bullying blog?

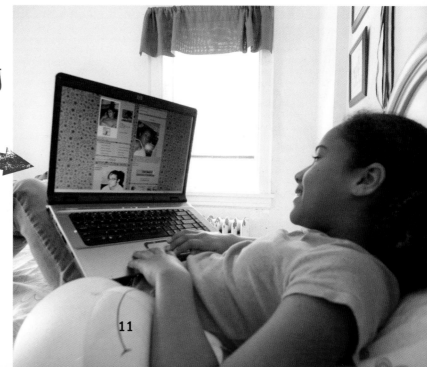

Internet Questions and Gaming

Formspring and other question-and-answer Web sites can be fun for asking questions and posting ideas. But what if someone posts a question like "Who's the ugliest kid in fifth grade?" That kind of question is hurtful. Other kids might take part in this kind of question and the bullying could spread. If you are the victim of a question like this, you may wonder who your real friends are.

Mean questions and comments online can sometimes turn into face-to-face bullying comments.

If another player posts bad language online, tell an adult right away.

Many kids play **interactive** games that are connected to the Internet. They can chat with one another online as they play the games. These games can be fun, but cyberbullies can ruin the experience for everyone. Bullies might taunt other players or use bad language. They might also steal passwords and lock other players out of their own accounts.

YouTube provides access to all kinds of different videos.

Bullying on Social Media Sites

Many adults and teens use Facebook and Twitter
to communicate with one another each day.
Some of these **social media** sites have rules
against younger kids using them. However, kids
sometimes use these sites anyway. There are sites
that are created just for younger users. These
include Yoursphere and giantHello. Kids also post
videos to YouTube and photos to Flickr.

With all these sites, it is important to know that they can be misused. A bully might write a hurtful post or comment that is seen by hundreds of other users all at once. Bullies can also post embarrassing photos. A bully might shoot a video that is mean and post that as well. If this happens to you or someone you care about, it can be very upsetting.

Facebook requires its users to be at least 13 years old.

One scary part of cyberbullying is that a bully's posts can reach many people very quickly.

16

CHAPTER 2

Why Cyberbullying Is So Serious

If someone writes you a mean note and leaves it in your locker, you're probably the only one who will see it. But the Internet does not work that way. Too often, hurtful messages can be posted for many people to see. A victim of cyberbullying may be really embarrassed by the messages. He or she may also feel scared and **depressed**.

A victim of cyberbullying can feel like other kids are ganging up on her.

Messaging Instantly

The Internet is easy to use, and most people use it every day. Messages travel almost instantly and can reach a lot of people. A negative post on a social media site can reach all of a victim's friends at once. So can an e-mail sent to everyone in a victim's address book. A video on YouTube can be viewed by thousands of people or more.

Online information can be accessed by anyone with an Internet connection. This can be a great chance to share ideas.

Writing a letter by hand can give you a better chance to think about what you're writing.

A handwritten letter might not be delivered for a few days. There is no delay at all for e-mails or other messages. They are delivered in a split second. Also, when people write letters by hand, they can think about what they are writing before sending the letters. They might even tear the letters up and not send them at all. With e-mail, people are more likely to type an angry message and hit Send before thinking about it.

Be careful about the information you share online. Make sure that you know the person you are talking to.

Who Is Saying What?

On the Internet, people usually have user names. You probably know your friends' and family's user names. But are you always sure who is really speaking? When people are online, they can often be **anonymous**. They can hide behind strange names, and you might not be sure to whom you're talking. When a message is hurtful or threatening, that uncertainty can be scary.

People who are good with computers know how to **hack** into other people's accounts. They might steal passwords and log on as other people. A hacker could use your e-mail or social media account and say mean things to other people, pretending to be you. Likewise, someone could pretend to be your best friend and send messages to you that are negative or threatening.

A good way to protect your account is to use a password that would be hard to guess. Mix up numbers, letters, and symbols in your password.

21

Cyberbullying Side Effects

When people are being cyberbullied, they may feel like everyone is against them. They may be scared or so embarrassed that they stop going to school or playing with friends. They can become depressed and withdrawn. Or they may become angry and fight back in violent ways. Either way, cyberbullying is serious. Just a few mean words can ruin people's lives.

Being cyberbullied can make a victim upset and angry. The victim might end up becoming a bully himself.

22

Cyberbullying Suicides

Cyberbullying has upset some victims so much that they committed **suicide**.

A 13-year-old named Ryan Patrick Halligan killed himself in 2003. He had received hurtful instant messages and was bullied at school.

In 2006, 13-year-old Megan Meier committed suicide. A friend's mother had created a fake Myspace profile, pretending to be a 16-year-old boy. She used the site to taunt Megan.

Fifteen-year-old Phoebe Prince had moved from Ireland to Massachusetts. In 2010, she killed herself after receiving nasty online messages and e-mails.

Bullying Can Happen 24/7

People who are bullied face-to-face know how awful the experience can be. They may feel scared and disliked. Cyberbullying can feel even worse. For its victims, the taunting can feel like it is everywhere and will never go away.

Online messages can be posted quickly and spread instantly.

Hundreds or even thousands of people can see embarrassing photos and videos that are posted online.

Using the Internet, bullies can taunt their victims anytime and anywhere—at home, on the weekends, at midnight, even on vacation.

While bullying at school usually stops when kids get home, online bullying is different. It can be constant, happening 24 hours a day. Victims may feel like they can't escape it.

Once something is spread online, it may never really be taken off the Internet.

It may be tempting to ignore cyberbullying and hope it goes away on its own. But it is important to take action against a cyberbully.

CHAPTER 3

How to Handle Cyberbullying

What do you think is the best way to handle cyberbullying? Should a victim ignore it? Think again. Anyone who is the victim of cyberbullying should take action. Bullies need to be stopped. This is as true for bullies on the Internet as for bullies on the playground. There is no reason to put up with this treatment.

If you don't stop cyberbullies, they may mistreat other people, too.

Reacting to Bullies

If you are being cyberbullied, you may not want to cause trouble. You may hope that if you ignore the problem, it will go away. This is not always true. If someone is using bad language or threatening you online, the police may need to become involved. The bullies may be breaking online rules or the law.

If cyberbullies are threatening you, it is important that you tell an adult.

Talking things over with an adult can help you figure out what to do about cyberbullying.

If you receive a cyberbullying message, do not send a fast, angry answer. Instead, walk away from your computer or cell phone. Tell a trusted friend or adult. You might feel most comfortable talking with your parent, your grandparent, a friend's parent, or even a neighbor. Ask the person for advice. Take time to think before answering the bully in any way.

You can block a cyberbully from your e-mail or phone. If a cyberbully is your friend on a social media site, you can delete that person from your friend list.

Know Your Friends

A person who cyberbullies you is not a friend, either online or in person. If you are being cyberbullied, block the bully from your sites. At the very least, don't answer the hurtful messages. There is no reason for you to argue with this person online. Instead, get the support of real friends.

Supportive friends are the best defense against cyberbullying. When you surround yourself with people you can count on, those nasty messages will be easier to handle. Remember that bullies are usually unhappy people who are just trying to act important. Friends won't let you believe any of the mean things bullies say.

The support of a few close friends can make a huge difference if you are being cyberbullied.

Asking for Help

Talk to a parent or another trusted adult if the cyberbullying seems serious. Bullying is serious if someone threatens you or if the messages are frequent. Don't worry about feeling like a tattletale if you feel scared or unsafe. Some cyberbullies will try to do harm. It is important that you protect yourself. It may also help to talk to a guidance counselor or school **psychologist** if you are upset.

Timeline of Cyberbullying

2003
In Vermont, Ryan Patrick Halligan kills himself after being bullied through instant messages.

2004
The social media site Facebook is launched.

If you have friends who are being cyberbullied, be sure they know you support them. Encourage them to talk about how they feel. Bullies can make their victims feel disliked and frightened. Make it clear to your friends that you care about them. Let them know that they can rely on you no matter what. If you think a friend is in danger, make sure you tell a trusted adult about what is going on.

2009
Formspring is launched as a social question-and-answer site.

2011
The White House holds its first Conference on Bullying Prevention.

2012
Facebook has more than 900 million users.

You and your friends can team up against cyberbullies and make the Internet a safer, friendlier tool to use.

CHAPTER 4

Ways to Stop Cyberbullying

It may be hard to stop cyberbullying altogether. Unfortunately, there will probably always be bullies both online and in person. But there are things you can do to help prevent cyberbullying. You can learn to protect yourself, your friends, and the people around you. You can also find ways to keep cyberbullying from becoming worse.

Cyberbullies may back off when they see how much support you have from friends.

Follow the Rules

Be sure you understand the rules that your parents have set for phone and Internet use. Some families limit the number of hours you can use them each day, or they limit the number of texts. Parents may also keep certain sites off-limits. Understand that if you

break these rules, you may be going somewhere on the Internet that is not safe.

Phone and Internet rules can help protect you from cyberbullies.

36

Your parents can help you find a fun, safe social media site to use to connect to friends.

Certain social media sites are not suitable for kids. Talk to your parents about the age rules for sites that you are interested in. For instance, site rules do not allow a 10-year-old to be on Facebook. There are plenty of other sites, such as Everloop or Imbee, that are designed for younger users. Explore different sites and see which ones you like best.

Online games can be great, but it can also be fun to play a game in person with your family.

Enjoy Life Off-line

These days, it's easy to get caught up in all the electronics. Online games are fun, and texting is fast and easy. However, remember that there is more to life than social media. Every day, take time to sign off and enjoy friends in person. Read a book or go to the movies. Play with your pets and have a meal with your family.

If cyberbullying has you questioning the good things about your life, stop and make a list. Write down all the great things about yourself, your home, your family, and your friends. If bullies have made you scared, try a new hobby. An activity like karate or tae kwon do can help you build strength and confidence.

Karate and other activities can help you gain confidence and make friends at the same time.

Have You Been a Cyberbully?

Think about how you act online or in text messages. Are you mean or rude? Before you send a message, stop and think. Would you say that same thing to someone in person? Reread the message. Do you really mean it? And how would you feel if someone said the same thing about you? Take time to think before posting photos and videos, too.

Never say or post anything online that you wouldn't say to someone in person.

Some Things Are Private!

Be careful about the information you post online.
Never give out your address or phone number.
People who are really your friends will already have
that information. Check your privacy settings. Set
those so that only your friends can see your posts.
Never give out your passwords. If you don't want
anyone but your best friend to know a secret, don't
post it online. Don't post things that embarrass
you or anyone else either. Remember who sees your
messages and updates.
If something is
private, keep it
that way!

If you are cyberbullied, be careful not to continue the cyberbullying by hurting other people.

If you have been bullied online, it may make you want to do it to other people as well. You might think it's a way to get back at the people who hurt you. But that kind of thinking just means that cyberbullying may never end! Instead, try to make the bullying stop. Remember how you felt when you were bullied. You don't want that for anyone else, do you?

Show Some Respect

If you are cyberbullied, show the bully that you **respect** yourself. If you know someone or see someone being cyberbullied, offer that person support and encouragement. Make it clear that you are not going to play the bully's game. Before you are tempted to bully others, give them respect. Don't make them feel scared or disliked. If we all respect one another, there will be no place for bullying—online or in person. ★

Make sure to treat yourself and the people around you and online with respect.

Percentage of teens and preteens who have been bullied online: About 50

Percentage of kids who have visited a Web site that criticizes another kid: 75

Number of kids who have had online passwords stolen by bullies who have locked them out of their accounts: 4 out of 10

Percentage of kids who tell their parents when they are cyberbullied: Almost 50

Number of kids who have had embarrassing photos taken of them without their permission (usually by a cell phone): 1 out of 10

Number of states that have passed bullying-prevention laws: 49

Did you find the truth?

T Not all social media sites are suitable for users of all ages.

F You always know who is talking when someone sends a message or posts online.

Resources

Books

Ludwig, Trudy. *Confessions of a Former Bully*. Berkeley, CA: Tricycle Press, 2010.

Murphy, Alexa Gordon. *Dealing With Bullying*. New York: Chelsea House, 2009.

Nelson, Drew. *Dealing With Cyberbullies*. New York: Gareth Stevens, 2013.

Peterson, Judy Monroe. *How to Beat Cyberbullying*. New York: Rosen Central, 2013.

Visit this Scholastic Web site for more information on cyberbullying:
★ www.factsfornow.scholastic.com
Enter the keyword **Cyberbullying**

Important Words

anonymous (uh-NAH-nuh-muhs) — not named or identified

depressed (di-PREST) — sad and unhappy with life

hack (HAK) — to secretly change or get into a computer system without permission

interactive (in-tur-AK-tiv) — allowing the users of a computer program to make choices in order to control or change features of the program

posted (POHST-id) — put messages, videos, photos, or other information on a Web site

psychologist (sye-KAH-luh-jist) — a person who studies people's minds and emotions and the ways that people behave

respect (ri-SPEKT) — to feel admiration or high regard for someone or something

rumors (ROO-murz) — stories or reports that are spread by word of mouth but may not be true

social media (SOH-shuhl MEE-dee-uh) — Web sites that help people connect with each other

suicide (SOO-i-side) — the act of killing oneself on purpose

taunt (TAWNT) — to try to make someone angry or upset by saying unkind things about him or her

victim (VIK-tuhm) — a person who is hurt, killed, or made to suffer

Index

Page numbers in **bold** indicate illustrations.

accounts, 8, 13, **21**
adults, 13, 14, 28, **29**, 32, 33
anonymity, **20**

blocking, **30**
blogs, **11**

cell phones, 7, **9**, 29
comments, 9, 10, 11, **12**, 15

definition, 7
depression, 17, 22

e-mails, **8**, 18, 19, 21, 23, **30**
embarrassment, 7, **10**, 15, 17, 22, 24, 41
Everloop, 37

Facebook, 14, **15**, **32**, 33, 37
fear, 17, 22, 24, 32, 39, 43
Flickr, 14
Formspring, 12, 33
friends, 12, 18, 29, 30–**31**, 33, **34**, 35, 38, **39**, 41

games, 13, **38**
giantHello, 14

hacking, 21
Halligan, Ryan Patrick, 23, **32**
hobbies, 10, **39**

Imbee, 37
instant messages, 23, 32
interactive games, 13
Internet, 7, **13**, 17, **18**, 20, 24, 25, 27, **34**, 36

language, **13**, 28

laws, 28
letters, **19**

Myspace, 23

off-line activities, **38–39**

parents, 29, 32, **36**, 37, **38**
passwords, 13, **21**, 41
personal information, 41
photos, **10**, 14, 15, 24, 40
police, 28
privacy, 41
psychologists, 32

respect, **43**
revenge, 42
rules, 14, 28, **36**–37
rumors, 11

scary feelings. *See* fear.
social media, 14, **15**, 18, 21, **32**, 33, **37**, 38
suicide, 23

taunting, 8, 10, 13, 23, 24
text messages, 7, 8, **9**, 36, 40
threats, 7, 9, 20, 21, 28, 32
timeline, **32–33**
Twitter, 14

user names, 20

video, **10**, **14**, 15, 18, 24, 40

Yoursphere, 14
YouTube, **14**, 18

About the Author

Lucia Raatma is a writer and editor who enjoys working on books for young readers. She earned a bachelor's degree in English from the University of South Carolina and a master's degree in cinema studies from New York University. She likes writing about all sorts of subjects, including history, conservation, wildlife, character education, and social media. She lives with her husband and their two children in the Tampa Bay area of Florida.